RASPBERRY PI
PROJECTS
WORKBOOK

Author and consultant Sway Grantham

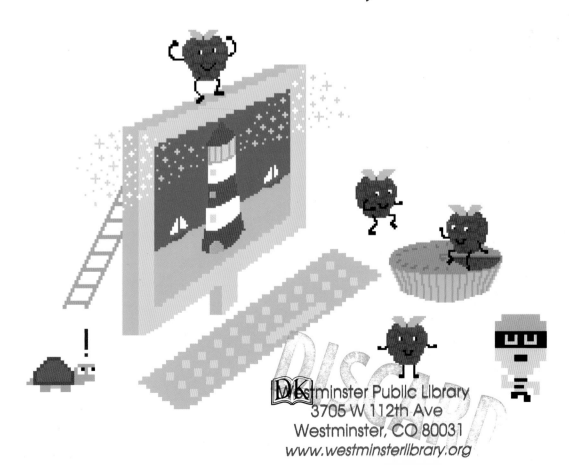

DK Westminster Public Library
3705 W 112th Ave
Westminster, CO 80031
www.westminsterlibrary.org

Written by
Sway Grantham
Editor Jolyon Goddard
Designer Peter Radcliffe
Project Art Editor Hoa Luc
US Editor Allison Singer
Jacket Coordinator Francesca Young
Jacket Designers Dheeraj Arora, Amy Keast
Proofreader Sarah Foakes
Managing Editor Laura Gilbert
Managing Art Editor Diane Peyton Jones
Pre-Production Producer Dragana Puvacic
Producer Niamh Tierney
Art Director Martin Wilson
Publisher Sarah Larter
Publishing Director Sophie Mitchell

First American Edition, 2017
Published in the United States by DK Publishing
345 Hudson Street, New York, New York 10014

A catalog record for this book
is available from the Library of Congress
ISBN: 978-1-4654-5703-5

DK books are available at special discounts when purchased in bulk for sales, promotions,
premiums, fund-raising, or educational use. For details, contact DK Publishing Special Markets,
345 Hudson Street, New York, New York 10014
SpecialSales@dk.com

Raspberry Pi and the Raspberry Pi logo are registered trademarks of the Raspberry Pi Foundation
in the United Kingdom and other countries. See https://www.raspberrypi.org

Scratch is developed by the Lifelong Kintergarten Group at MIT Media Lab.
See https://scratch.mit.edu

Sonic Pi was created by Sam Aaron at the University of Cambridge Computer Laboratory with
kind support from the Raspberry Pi Foundation. See http://sonic-pi.net

Python is copyright © 2001–2017 Python Software Foundation; All Rights Reserved. The Python
Software Foundation is entirely open source and maintained by volunteers. Many thanks to Guido
van Rossum and the thousands of volunteer programmers who work on the Python language.

Picture Credits
The publisher would like to thank the following for their kind permission to reproduce their photographs:
(Key: b=below, c=center, r=right)
6 Getty Images: Olly Curtis/Future Publishing (b). **9 Debian:** https://www.debian.org (crb).

All other images © Dorling Kindersley
For further information see: www.dkimages.com

Printed and bound in China

A WORLD OF IDEAS:
SEE ALL THERE IS TO KNOW

www.dk.com

Contents

Raspberry Pi lineup

Have you ever seen a Raspberry Pi? There are lots of different models, and they do many amazing things. Some of the smaller models are great for putting inside other things, such as spy cameras. Other models can control robots, make games for you to play, and much more!

What is a Raspberry Pi?

A Raspberry Pi is a mini computer that doesn't cost very much. It is designed to help children learn the basics of computing and programming, and its small size makes it useful for many different projects. The Raspberry Pi looks very different from other computers; it comes without a case, so you can see its microchips and circuit board.

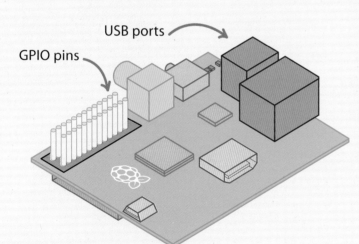

USB ports

GPIO pins

◀ The original Model B

This is an old Raspberry Pi model. The telltale sign is that there are only two USB ports and 26 GPIO pins. If you find one of these, it will still work, but it'll be slower than the newer models.

▶ Pi 3

This is the latest version of the Model B and the best to use when you're getting started and learning how to program. The Pi 3 comes with Wi-Fi (wireless internet) and Bluetooth. Two earlier versions—Model B+ and Pi 2—look very similar to the Pi 3. Ask an adult to help you make sure you get the right model if you want a Pi 3.

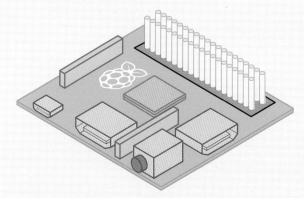

◀ Model A+

This almost-square Raspberry Pi model is great for projects that need a smaller computer. It's not as fast as the Pi 3 and doesn't have built-in Wi-Fi to connect it to the Internet. It uses less power than the bigger models, which is useful if you need to use batteries to power it.

▶ Pi Zero

This model is the cheapest and smallest of the Pi family. It needs adapters to be able to connect to a keyboard and mouse. It doesn't have GPIO pins, but you can solder them on. The Pi Zero is best suited to really small projects.

You can solder on GPIO pins here

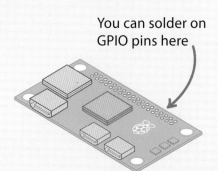

Read me!

This book is based on using the latest—at the time of writing—model of the Raspberry Pi, which is the **Pi 3**. Some of the projects in this book may not work with other models of Raspberry Pi.

Challenge
Now that you've learned about the different Raspberry Pi models, which model do you think would be best for each project below?

Project 1: Use a Pi to make a burglar alarm to guard your class's secret treasure. (**Hint:** You will need a small model with GPIO pins.)

....

Project 2: Use a Pi to control a small teddy bear so that it works like a robot. (**Hint:** You will need a very small model to fit inside your teddy bear.)

....

Project 3: Use a Pi to make an insect observatory that records what bugs get up to when no one's around, and share the photographs on the school website. (**Hint:** You will need a Pi with Wi-Fi to send the photographs.)

....

Getting connected

A Raspberry Pi is a simple computer, but it won't do anything on its own. It needs electricity to run, but even powered up, how do you know what it's doing? How do you make it do what you want? Let's take a closer look at the ports, or connection points, on the Raspberry Pi 3.

▼ Raspberry Pi 3

A Raspberry Pi 3 has many ports. Some are for inputs, and others are for outputs. Inputs, such as a keyboard and mouse, allow you to control the computer and make it do what you want. Outputs, such as a monitor and speakers, let you know what the computer is doing.

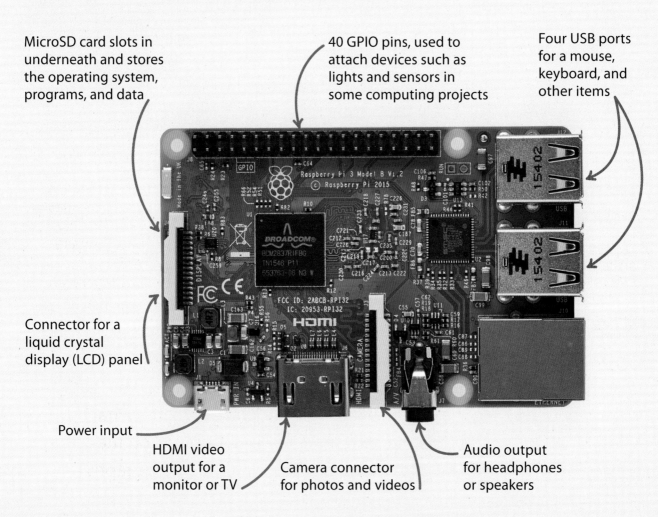

MicroSD card slots in underneath and stores the operating system, programs, and data

40 GPIO pins, used to attach devices such as lights and sensors in some computing projects

Four USB ports for a mouse, keyboard, and other items

Connector for a liquid crystal display (LCD) panel

Power input

HDMI video output for a monitor or TV

Camera connector for photos and videos

Audio output for headphones or speakers

What do I need to use a Raspberry Pi?

A Raspberry Pi is easy to use, but it needs the following accessories to get up and running:

- A keyboard
- A mouse
- A monitor or TV
- A microSD card and SD card adapter
- A micro USB power adapter
- An HDMI cable

You will also need access to a computer with an SD card reader and writer.

Other accessories, such as cameras, speakers, and headphones, can be added depending on what you want to do with your Raspberry Pi. You can even connect lights, buzzers, and sensors if you use the GPIO pins.

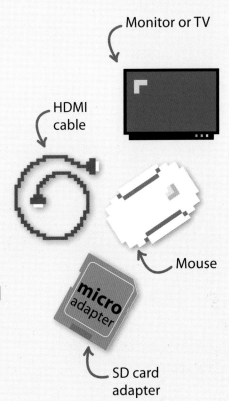

Monitor or TV

HDMI cable

Mouse

micro adapter

SD card adapter

Keep it clean!

To keep your Pi dust-free and clean, you can make your own protective case. Some people build it out of LEGO or make a small box from cardboard—just remember to leave holes in it for air vents!

Connecting your Raspberry Pi

When you connect your Pi, always connect the electricity last of all.

1. Put the microSD card in the card slot.
2. Plug the keyboard and mouse into the USB ports.
3. Use the HDMI cable to connect the Pi to a monitor or TV.
4. Connect to the power supply.

MicroSD card

Your Raspberry Pi might have come with a microSD card with software called **NOOBS** on it. NOOBS lets you install **Raspbian**, Raspberry Pi's main operating system. Pages 8–9 will tell you about installing NOOBS onto your card, if you don't already have it, and what to do when your Raspberry Pi loads for the first time.

Getting Raspbian

You're almost there—but if you haven't used your Raspberry Pi before, you'll have to install an operating system on your microSD card. The operating system is the place where all the programs you need are run from. The Pi's main operating system is called **Raspbian**.

You'll need NOOBS

Sometimes a Raspberry Pi comes with a microSD card that has NOOBS on it. NOOBS stands for **New Out Of the Box Software**, and it contains Raspbian. If your card already has NOOBS on it, skip ahead to **Using your Pi for the first time**, on the opposite page. If you have a brand-new microSD card without NOOBS, read the instructions below.

Downloading NOOBS

To download NOOBS onto your microSD card, you will need to use a computer, such as a laptop, with an SD card reader and writer.

1. First, slide your microSD card into the SD card adapter. These adapters are usually sold with microSD cards. Then put the SD card adapter, with the microSD card in it, into the laptop's SD card slot.

2. When it's in the slot, go to the **NOOBS** page of the Raspberry Pi Foundation's website (www.raspberrypi.org/downloads/noobs). You now need to download the zip file called **NOOBS—Offline and network install**.

3. When it's finished, copy the files from the zip file onto your microSD card. There should be about 15 files and a few folders to copy over.

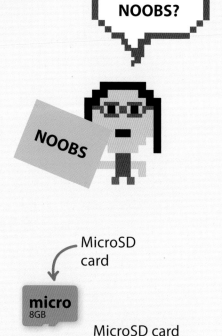

What's NOOBS?

NOOBS

MicroSD card

micro
8GB

MicroSD card slots in here

micro adapter

SD card adapter

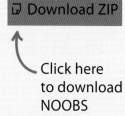

▢ Download ZIP

Click here to download NOOBS

4. Take the SD card adapter out of the laptop, and then take the microSD card out of the adapter. Now set up your Pi as described in **Connecting your Raspberry Pi** on page 7, remembering to connect the power supply last of all.

Slot your microSD card into your Pi

Using your Pi for the first time

The first time you use a new microSD card in a Raspberry Pi, it will need to install the operating system Raspbian. The latest version—at the time of writing this book—is called **Jessie**, and it contains all the software, including Scratch, Sonic Pi, and IDLE, that you need to get programming.

1. After connecting your Pi to the power supply, you should see a rainbow-colored screen and then something similar to the screen shown here.

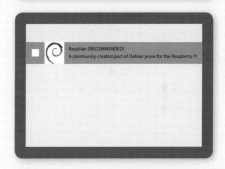

2. The computer will then ask you what you want to install, and you will need to check the operating system Raspbian and then click on **Install**.

3. Finally, it will ask for your permission for it to install Raspbian, and you need to click on **Yes**.

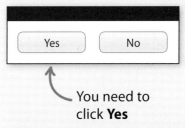

You need to click **Yes**

Now it will get to work making your Pi ready to use. This will take a little time, and there will be some messages that scroll across the screen while it's working. When it's finished, you will see a desktop screen similar to this. Now you're ready to work through the activities in this book!

Jailbreak

You are on your way to a costume party dressed as a robber when someone mistakes you for a *real* robber and throws you in jail! You must now escape through the jail's maze of corridors before you're locked in for the night.

What you'll learn:
• How to control a sprite using the arrow keys
• How to set a countdown timer using a variable
• How to stop a sprite from walking through walls

Sprite always starts here

Door that you need to get to before the time reaches 15 seconds

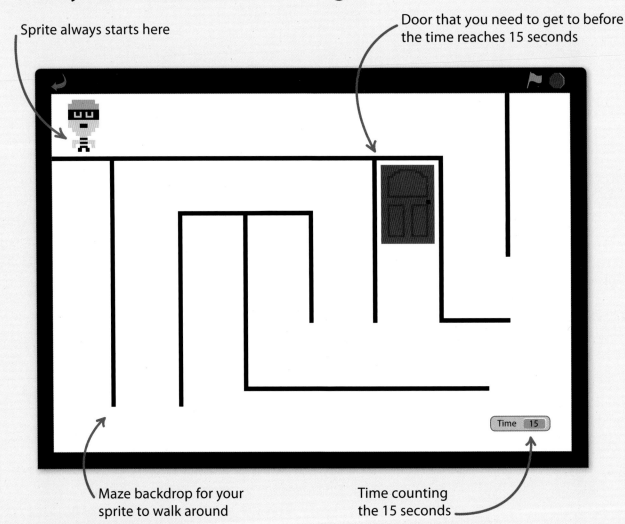

Maze backdrop for your sprite to walk around

Time counting the 15 seconds

▲ Playing the game

To program this activity, you need to open Scratch Version 1.4, which you can find under **Programming** on the Raspberry Pi **Menu**. When playing, use the arrow keys to move your robber sprite. Don't touch the walls or you'll go back to the beginning. You do need to rush, though: If you don't get to the door in 15 seconds, you will lose!

Decomposition

When starting to write a computer program, you should think about breaking it in down into small steps. This process is called **decomposition**, and it means that you can work in small chunks, such as the 13 steps described in this game, and build up to the complete program.

Create a sprite

To get started, you need to create a sprite and get it to follow simple instructions called **scripts**. You also need to design a jail maze. Be as creative as you want!

1 If you have just opened Scratch, you should see the cat in the middle of your screen. You don't need him for this project, so right-click and delete him to make room for your robber sprite.

Robber sprite

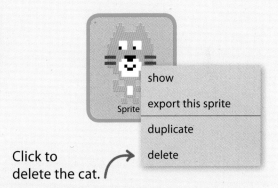

Sprite

show

export this sprite

Click to
delete the cat.

duplicate

delete

2 Now you need a robber sprite. Here you have two choices. You can click on **Choose new sprite from file** if you already have a robber picture you'd like to use saved on your Raspberry Pi. Or, you can click on **Paint new sprite** if you want to draw your own robber.

Sprites

Sprites are characters that you can program. Sometimes you will want to program them to move and be controlled by the user. At other times you might just want to give them their own instructions. Always make sure you have clicked on the sprite that you want to program before you start your script.

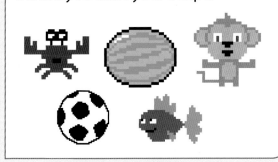

3 Let's make your robber sprite move. First of all, you will need this **Control** block, which tells the computer when to do something.

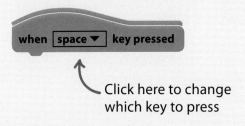

when space ▼ key pressed

Click here to change
which key to press

4 The computer now knows that it needs to do something when a key is pressed, but it doesn't know what to do. You need to tell it to move up, down, left, and right when the arrow keys are pressed. Build these coordinate instructions in the robber sprite's scripts area.

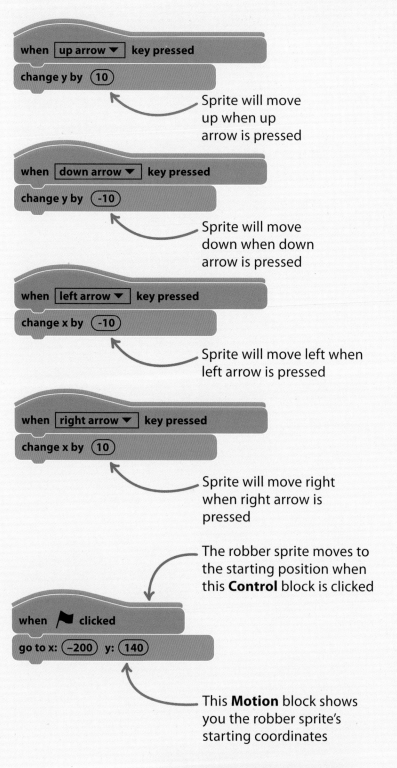

when [up arrow ▼] key pressed
change y by (10)

Sprite will move up when up arrow is pressed

when [down arrow ▼] key pressed
change y by (-10)

Sprite will move down when down arrow is pressed

when [left arrow ▼] key pressed
change x by (-10)

Sprite will move left when left arrow is pressed

when [right arrow ▼] key pressed
change x by (10)

Sprite will move right when right arrow is pressed

x and y coordinates

Do you ever forget which is the x coordinate and which is the y coordinate? All you need to remember is the letter **x** has two lines that **cross** and it goes **across**, so any x coordinate is going to go left or right. To remember which way the y coordinate goes, think about putting your hand up to ask "**why**?" and you'll know **y** goes up or down.

5 Copy this code. It places the robber sprite in the same position every time the game starts. Use the coordinates shown here in the **go to x:__ y:__** block. If you want to change this position, hover your mouse in the place you want to start and you'll see the coordinates you need in the bottom-right corner of the game window. Then type those coordinates into the block.

when ⚑ clicked
go to x: (-200) y: (140)

The robber sprite moves to the starting position when this **Control** block is clicked

This **Motion** block shows you the robber sprite's starting coordinates

Check-in

If you try running your program now, your robber sprite should start in the same place every time and then move around the screen when you press the arrow keys.

Debugging

It's easy to make mistakes when building scripts. Check them carefully if they don't work. Fixing mistakes in code is called **debugging**.

6 You now need to draw the walls of your jail. Make sure there's enough space between the walls so that your robber sprite can move around without touching them. Click on **Stage**, then **Backgrounds**, and then **Edit**. Use the **Line tool** in **Paint Editor** to create your own maze. Then check your sprite can get around it by using the arrow keys.

Robber sprite

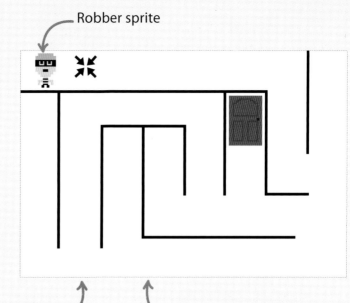

Maze

Make sure you leave enough space for the robber sprite to move around between the lines

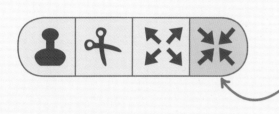

If your robber sprite is too large, reduce it using the **Shrink** tool

Will I ever be free?

7 You now need a door, through which your robber can escape. Even though the door won't move, it will still be a sprite. To make a door sprite, click on **Choose new sprite from file** or **Paint new sprite**, just as you did in Step 2 to make the robber sprite.

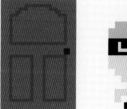

8 Now that you have two sprites, it's a good idea to rename them. This stops them from getting mixed up by accident. To do this, click on the sprite and type the new name in the name box above the scripts area.

Rename your two sprites **Door** and **Robber**

Check-in

You will now be able to move your robber sprite around the maze and see the door. You can move the door in the stage area to where you want it to be in the maze.

Giving the sprite rules

Your robber sprite can now move, but there's a problem—it can walk through the walls to get to the door! That's not very realistic. You now need to give the sprite some rules.

I love walking through walls!

9 Program the robber sprite so that when it touches a wall it's sent back to the beginning. To do this, you need to add an **if** block from the **Control** section to your script from Step 5. You will need a **forever** loop, too, which will check "forever" if the robber sprite touches a wall.

This square needs to be the same color as the jail walls. To make the colors match, first click on the square and then click on a wall.

Starts the program

Puts the robber at the start position

Keeps checking "forever"

Adds a one-second penalty for touching a wall

Checks if the robber sprite touches a wall

If the robber sprite touches a wall, it is sent back to the start

```
when ⚑ clicked
go to x: (-200) y: (140)
forever
    if  < touching color ■ ? >
        go to x: (-200) y: (140)
        wait (1) secs
```

10 The **forever** loop checks if the robber sprite touches a wall. However, it doesn't check if the robber has reached the door. You now need to add another **if** block to your script from Step 9, but this time you want to check if the robber is touching the door, and end the game if it is.

Add this block to make the robber reappear if you want to play again after making it through the door on the previous turn

Makes the robber disappear if it reaches the door

When the robber touches the door, everything stops and the game ends

Checks if the robber is touching the door

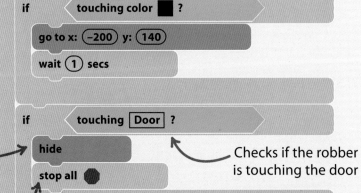

```
when ⚑ clicked
show
go to x: (-200) y: (140)
forever
    if  < touching color ■ ? >
        go to x: (-200) y: (140)
        wait (1) secs
    if  < touching [Door] ? >
        hide
        stop all ⬢
```

Check-in

If you try running your program now, you should be sent back to the starting position if your robber sprite touches a wall. Also, if the robber sprite reaches the door, it should disappear through it.

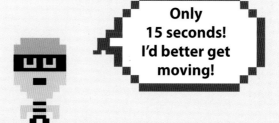

Setting a time limit

The game now looks good, but it's easy. Everyone can get to the door eventually. So let's now set a time limit.

11 Click on **Variables**, then on **Make a variable**, and name it **Time**. This will save how long it has been since the game started. If you check the box next to the variable, it will appear in the game window. Now start building a new script for your robber sprite using a **when flag clicked** block from the **Control** section and **set Time to** block from the **Variables** section.

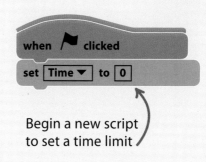

Begin a new script to set a time limit

12 Add more blocks to your new script. The time will now increase by 1 every second, and the **forever** loop will make this go on "forever" until you tell it when to stop—in the next step.

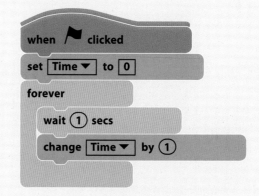

Check-in

Try running your program again. You should see the time box counting each second.

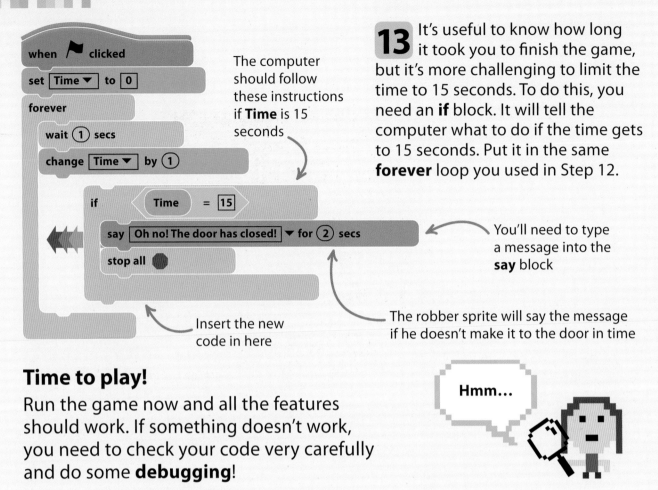

13 It's useful to know how long it took you to finish the game, but it's more challenging to limit the time to 15 seconds. To do this, you need an **if** block. It will tell the computer what to do if the time gets to 15 seconds. Put it in the same **forever** loop you used in Step 12.

The computer should follow these instructions if **Time** is 15 seconds

You'll need to type a message into the **say** block

The robber sprite will say the message if he doesn't make it to the door in time

Insert the new code in here

Time to play!

Run the game now and all the features should work. If something doesn't work, you need to check your code very carefully and do some **debugging**!

Hmm…

Show what you know

Now that you've escaped from jail, try these challenges.

1. What is it called when you take a problem and break it into small steps?

....

2. Can you use your skills to make the following improvements to the game?

a. Add an instructions sprite at the beginning. (**Hint:** You will need to program it to show at the beginning and hide when the game starts.)

b. Change the door sprite's costume so it looks different when open and when closed. (**Hint:** Change the costume if the time variable is at 15.)

c. Change the size of the robber sprite using the shrink or grow buttons to make the game simpler or harder.

3. Challenge yourself to make another game that's similar. In Scratch, this is called **remixing**. Remix ideas can include a mouse getting to some cheese, a knight getting to a castle, or an alien getting to its spaceship.

Sound symphony

Let your creative juices flow as you write your own music. Do you want to get everybody dancing, or would you rather compose a spine-tingling soundtrack for a spooky movie? Let's hear what you can do.

What you'll learn:
- How to use repetition in programs
- How to use random number generators
- How to edit a live program

You write code in this window

Click these arrows to get to useful options such as **Prefs** and **Help**

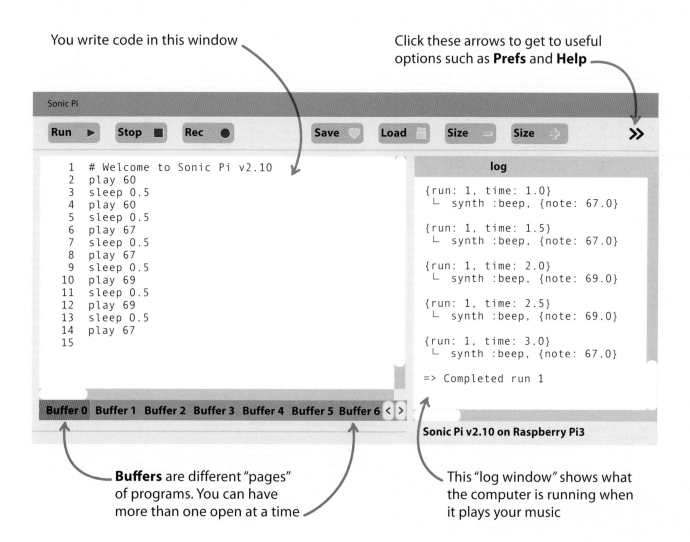

Buffers are different "pages" of programs. You can have more than one open at a time

This "log window" shows what the computer is running when it plays your music

▲ What you'll use

For this activity, you need to open Sonic Pi, Version 2.10, which can be found under **Programming** on the Raspberry Pi **Menu**. There's no "right" or "wrong" when programming music. You can create whatever you want to—but it's best to start with simple tunes before building up to orchestral pieces!

Making sure you have sound

Before you make any music, you need to check that you have sound. Revisit page 6 to see where you connect your headphones or speakers to your Raspberry Pi, so you can hear the sounds you're making. To test it, write **play 70** in the code window and click on **Run**.

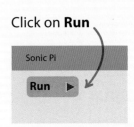

Click on **Run**

Sonic Pi

Run ▶

```
=> Starting run 1

{run: 1, time: 0.0}
 └ synth :beep, {note: 70.0}

=> Completed run 1
```

The log window should tell you that it is playing note 70. More importantly, you should be able to hear the note through your headphones or speakers.

If you do not hear anything, click on **Run** again and check the volume of the speakers or that the headphones are pushed in properly. If you still don't hear it, click on **Prefs**—you might need to click on those arrows first to make **Prefs** visible if your screen is small. Then select **Headphones** if you're using headphones, or **HDMI** if the other options don't work. Rerun your code, and you should now hear the note.

If you can't hear the note, try changing the audio output and running your code again

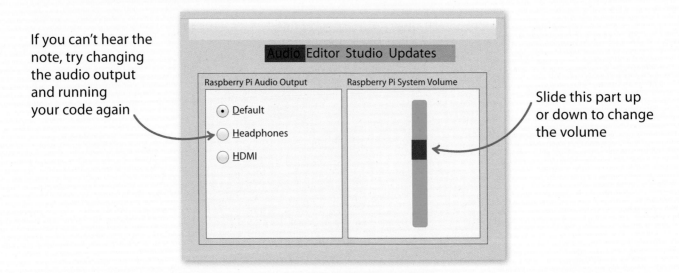

Audio Editor Studio Updates

Raspberry Pi Audio Output

⦿ Default
◯ Headphones
◯ HDMI

Raspberry Pi System Volume

Slide this part up or down to change the volume

Check-in

You now should hear a single beep when you run your code.

How does Sonic Pi work?

There are two ways of playing a note in Sonic Pi. You've already tried by writing a number. The other way is to write the musical note as a letter.

1 Delete the code you wrote when testing for sound, and now write this code. The notes should sound exactly the same. You can use whichever way you find easier, but for the rest of this activity you'll be coding using numbers.

```
play 60
sleep 1
play :c
```

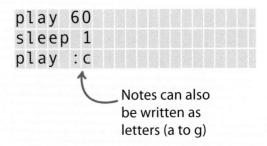

Notes can also be written as letters (a to g)

2 Now delete the last line of your code from Step 1 and add more lines, as shown here. Run the code and listen. You'll notice that as the number gets higher, the note gets higher, too.

The **sleep** instruction adds a pause between notes

```
play 60
sleep 1
play 62
sleep 1
play 64
sleep 1
play 66
```

Check-in

You should now be able to play basic notes. Experiment with different numbers. What's the biggest number you can use, and what's the smallest? Can you use numbers that aren't whole numbers, such as 60.5 or 78.3?

3 Delete the code you've written or click on a new **Buffer**. Now copy this code. Do you recognize the tune?

All together now!

If not, add the next notes: 65, 65, 64, 64, 62, 62, 60. You'll then probably realize it's "Twinkle, Twinkle, Little Star."

```
play 60
sleep 0.5
play 60
sleep 0.5
play 67
sleep 0.5
play 67
sleep 0.5
play 69
sleep 0.5
play 69
sleep 0.5
play 67
```

4 Now try making your own tune. Change the notes and the **sleep** time, which is the gap between the notes, and see what happens.

Starting a beat

A part of music that is really important is repetition. Good music usually has a beat or other parts that repeat over and over again until the tune's stuck in your head!

5 Copy the code on the right. It creates a synth beat that uses a loop to repeat two notes over and over again. Loops are common in programming and save you from the boring task of having to write the same lines over and over.

Helpful hint

You can keep all your different pieces of music. Each of the **Buffers** at the bottom of Sonic Pi saves your work. If a tune you've just finished is in **Buffer 0**, then just click on **Buffer 1** to start a new tune. Click on **Buffer 0** whenever you want to go back and hear it again or play it for friends.

A **live_loop** can be edited (changed) while your code is running

This part of the music is repeated. It is indented (moved over), which lets you see which part is repeated

```
live_loop :beat do
  use_synth :blade
  play 50
  sleep 0.5
  play 58
  sleep 0.5
end
```

The **blade** synth sound has a lot of vibration

beat is the name of the loop

Helpful hint

When using a **live_loop**, you must remember the **sleep** command before the end of your loop. Without it, the computer will try to play the same note over and over again as quickly as it can, and this causes it to crash because it can't keep up!

6 Below your code from Step 5, add a new loop that will repeat a melody you've written.

Adding a melody

Now you have the repeated beat in the background, you will want to add something to it that's a little more melodic!

```
live_loop :beat do
  use_synth :blade
  play 50
  sleep 0.5
  play 58
  sleep 0.5
end

live_loop :melody do
  use_synth :piano



end
```

melody is the name of the loop. You can use lots of **live_loops** in your program, but you must give them all different names

Put your own musical notes here to create your own melody. Don't forget to add the **sleep** commands

Adding atmosphere

You might want to create a piece of music for a special reason. Sonic Pi is great for that. Imagine you want a repeating sound that gives your music a spooky atmosphere. In Sonic Pi, there are several samples, which are small chunks of prerecorded music, that you can use.

I love those spooky sounds!

7 Copy this code and run it. It mixes spooky samples with normal notes. Try other combinations to make it even more spine-chilling!

```
live_loop :spooky do
  sample :ambi_dark_woosh
  sleep 2
  play 62
  sleep 0.5
  sample :ambi_drone
  sleep 2
  play 58
  sleep 0.5
end
```

Check-in

You can now use samples with musical notes to create different musical styles. Take time exploring the different samples. If you type **sample :** Sonic Pi will suggest a list of sounds you can use. Test each one, and decide which you like.

Making it unpredictable

Sometimes you don't want to hear the same thing again and again. If you're composing music for a spooky movie, you might want it to be unpredictable to keep your audience on edge. To do this, you use a command called **play rrand**, which picks a random note.

8 Look at the spooky code you wrote in Step 7. Try improving it by changing one of the **play** instructions to **play rrand**.

```
live_loop :spooky do
  play rrand(50, 85)
  sleep 0.5
end
```

This instruction is a random note generator

The computer randomly chooses from notes between 50 and 85

That music's totally random!

Check-in

When you are running your code, you can always see what the computer is doing in the log window to the right of where you type in your code. If you're using random commands, you'll be able to see which numbers the computer has chosen.

9 You can also use the random instruction to change how much **sleep** there is between notes. Try this code and run it.

The computer randomly chooses an amount of sleep between 0.5 and 2 seconds long

```
live_loop :spooky do
  play 62
  sleep rrand(0.5, 2)
end
```

Saving your music

When you have created your composition, you may want to save it. Saving it as a wavefile will let you be able to share it with friends or use it as the soundtrack to a movie you're making!

Turns pink when recording

10 To save a piece of music, click on the record button (**Rec**) and it will change to pink. Now run your music. When you've reached the end, press the record button again to turn it off. A box will then come up for you to save the piece. Name it and then click on **Save** at the bottom. The file will appear on your desktop.

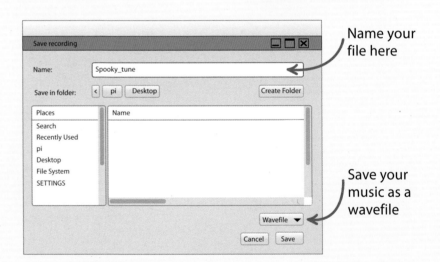

Name your file here

Save your music as a wavefile

Live coding

One of the most exciting things you can do with Sonic Pi is program music live. This means that while you're busy writing the code, your friends can be dancing to the music it makes at the same time!

11 Type in this code and run it. Live_loops are perfect for live coding because you can edit and add to them while they are playing.

```
live_loop :dancing do
  use_synth :tb303
  play 50
  sleep 0.25
end
```

12 While the code from Step 11 is playing, type in this second **live_loop** below it.

```
live_loop :newtune do
  use_synth :zawa
  play 80
  sleep 0.25
end
```

13 If you press **Run** or **alt-R** while the first code is still running, you'll hear the music changing at an appropriate point. Try adding a **play rrand** or sample. You could even edit the first **live_loop**. Again, press **Run** or **alt-R** to hear the changes.

Check-in
You should now be confident enough to program different types of music, from simple tunes to complicated pieces that include loops and samples. You should even be able to edit your music while playing it live!

Time to play!
Now start programming a piece of music that uses everything you have learned!

Show what you know
Build up your Sonic Pi skills by trying these extra challenges.

1. Create a familiar tune, such as 64, 62, 60, 62, 64, 64, 64, 62, 62, 62, 64, 67, 67. Don't forget the **sleep** commands!

2. Program a catchy chorus section that plays every 20 seconds while the rest of your music continues.

3. Can you debug, or spot and fix the mistakes in, these two programs?

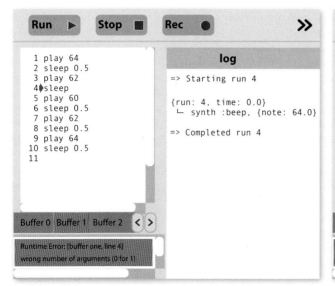

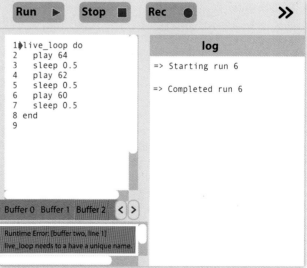

Crazy patterns

So far you've used your Raspberry Pi to create a fun game and program different types of music. Now it's time to do some art and make eye-catching patterns based on repeating just one simple shape. You'll be amazed what you can do!

What you'll learn:
• How to use the Python turtle library
• How to program simple shapes
• How to repeat simple shapes to create patterns

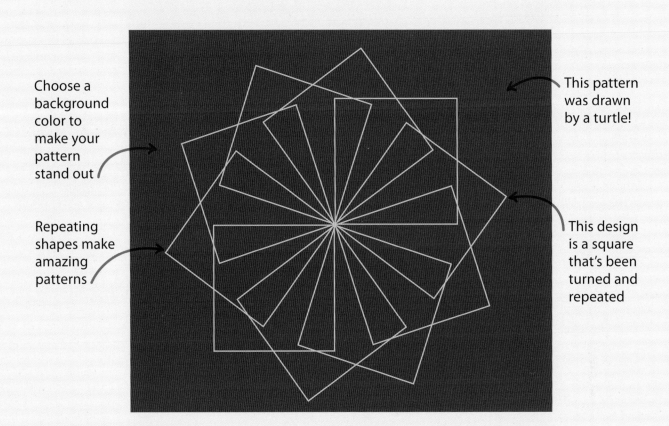

Choose a background color to make your pattern stand out

Repeating shapes make amazing patterns

This pattern was drawn by a turtle!

This design is a square that's been turned and repeated

▲ What you'll do

For this activity, you'll need to open the programming language **Python 3 (IDLE)**. It can be found under **Programming** on the Raspberry Pi **Menu**. Programming languages have lots of instructions that computers understand, so to make it easier the instructions are sorted into groups called "libraries." You will use a Python library called "turtle," which lets you program an onscreen character, or turtle, to draw.

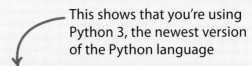

This shows that you're using Python 3, the newest version of the Python language

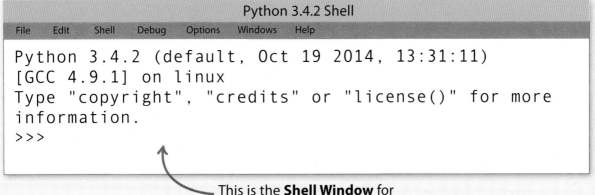

This is the **Shell Window** for seeing what your code is doing and any errors that appear

Using Python 3 (IDLE)

When you click on Python 3 (IDLE), you will see a basic text window like the one shown above. This is the **Shell Window**, and it shows you what your program is doing. It also shows you error messages if you have made mistakes when writing your program. You now want to create an **Editor Window**, to save the code you write. To do this, click **File** and then **New File**.

Click on **File** first, and then **New File**

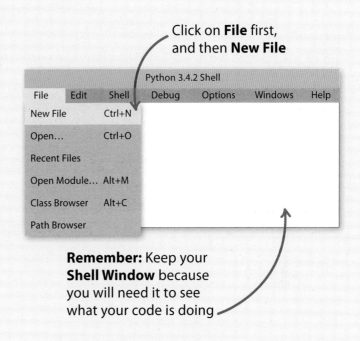

Remember: Keep your **Shell Window** because you will need it to see what your code is doing

Two windows

You might want to resize the two windows and put them near each other to begin with, so you can see what both are doing. The easiest way to do this is to move the mouse cursor to any edge or corner until you get a double-headed arrow. Now drag the window until it's the size you want. Once resized, position the windows how you want them.

Move windows where you want them to be

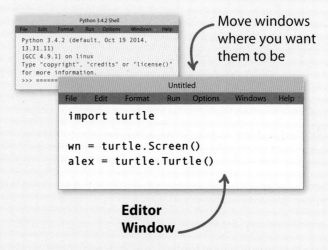

Editor Window

Starting to draw

There are some basic commands you need to know to get started, and then you can get to work creating your first piece of programmed art. All the typing you do should be in the **Editor Window**.

He wants to see alex the turtle!

Python rules

● Always spell things the way the computer thinks you should spell them. If something isn't working, look at what you've typed because it's very easy to make mistakes.

● Capital letters make a difference, so copy code exactly as it's written. Look at the line below that includes **turtle.Turtle()**—one turtle has a capital and other doesn't. You must copy it exactly as it is.

● Names such as "alex" don't usually have capital letters. This is the opposite of what your teachers tell you, but computer languages such as Python have their own rules!

● Check the spaces between each letter or symbol carefully when copying code. Sometimes spaces are needed and sometimes they aren't.

This code lets you use the commands in the turtle library

1 Type in these three lines of code. Run it (see Steps 5–6) and you'll see a new window pop up with a little shape like an arrowhead (▶) in the middle. That arrowhead is our turtle, alex.

```
import turtle

wn = turtle.Screen()
alex = turtle.Turtle()
```

This creates a turtle named "alex," which you can give instructions to

2 Now type **alex.forward (150)** on a new line and run it. This draws a straight line. 150 is the number of pixels alex will move. A pixel is a tiny square-shaped dot on a computer screen. So even though 150 seems like a big number, the line is not very long!

wn means "window" and refers to the window you will see your art in

```
import turtle

wn = turtle.Screen()
alex = turtle.Turtle()

alex.forward(150)
```

3 Now add the line **alex.left (90)** and run it. This new instruction will turn alex 90 degrees to his left. That's the same as a right angle.

```
import turtle

wn = turtle.Screen()
alex = turtle.Turtle()

alex.forward(150)
alex.left(90)
```

4 You can now use these two instructions to draw a square. You need to repeat those last two lines of code three more times, and run it. **Remember:** Follow the spellings, capital letters, and punctuation exactly as shown.

Check-in
You should now be able to program alex to draw lines, turn 90 degrees to make a corner, and draw a square.

5 To run your code, go to **Run** at the top of the **Editor Window**, and then click on **Run Module**. You can also press the key **F5**.

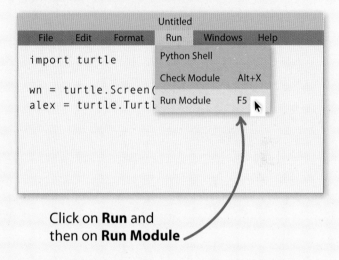

Click on **Run** and then on **Run Module**

6 You will now be asked to save it. In written programming languages, programs can't run without being saved. So give your file a name, such as **Art**, and save it.

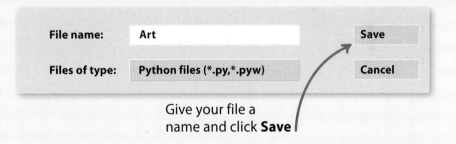

Give your file a name and click **Save**

A new window

As soon as you press **Save**, your code will run. Your **Shell Window** should say "RESTART" because you have told it to run something new. A new window called **Python Turtle Graphics** will pop up, and alex will draw whatever you have programmed. If it doesn't work, you need to check your code for mistakes!

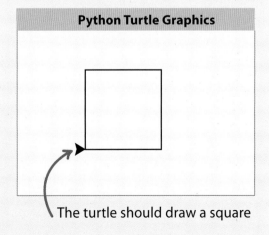

The turtle should draw a square

Using a loop

Writing the code for a square wasn't too bad. After all, it only had four sides, but did you really need to write the same thing again and again? In the previous projects in this book, you used a piece of code called a loop to repeat an instruction. You can also use loops in Python.

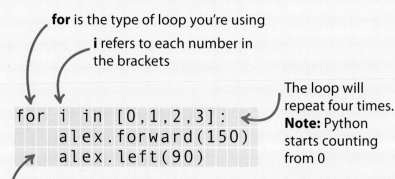

for is the type of loop you're using

i refers to each number in the brackets

```
for i in [0,1,2,3]:
    alex.forward(150)
    alex.left(90)
```

The loop will repeat four times. **Note:** Python starts counting from 0

A gap called an indent shows the instructions you want to repeat in the loop

7 Instead of the last eight lines you wrote before to draw a square, copy these three lines. It uses a **for loop** and makes the amount of typing you need to do a lot less! To make a gap called an indent in the code you want to repeat, press the **Tab** key, left of the key **Q** (if the indent doesn't appear automatically).

Check-in

You should now be able to use a **for loop** to repeat an instruction a number of times in Python.

Making Patterns

Now you're going to use loops to program exciting patterns such as the one shown here. This pattern looks tricky, but really it is just a square that is repeated several times. Figuring out how to do something complicated by breaking it down into small steps is called **decomposition**.

The code for this pattern draws a square, turns alex a number of degrees, draws another square, and so on, until it gets all the way around

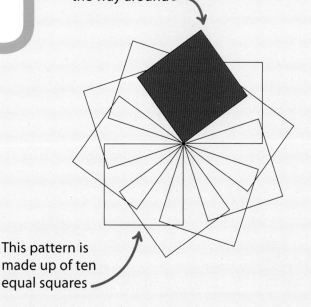

This pattern is made up of ten equal squares

8 Copy the code shown here, which adds a second **for loop**. Make sure to indent where shown. The final instruction for alex doesn't happen inside the square loop and needs to be underneath the **for** command three lines above.

This command repeats the code for drawing a square 10 times

```
for i in [0,1,2,3,4,5,6,7,8,9]:
    for i in [0,1,2,3]:
        alex.forward(150)
        alex.left(90)
alex.right(36)
```

This line turns alex 36 degrees each time he draws a square. Without it, alex would draw the square 10 times in the same place, and you would see only one square!

This is the code you already have for drawing a square

I'm going loopy!

Check-in

You should now have programmed two **for loops** to run together. This is called a "nested" loop. One loop creates the square, and the other loop makes more squares, each after a small turn.

9 Now change your code so that only five squares are drawn. You'll need to change the first **for loop** line to **for i in [0,1,2,3,4]:** and then the number of degrees in the bottom line to 72, so it's **alex. right(72)**

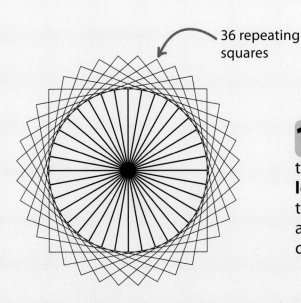

36 repeating squares

Five repeating squares

10 Try one more design, shown left. It's still a square in a loop, but this time the square repeats 36 times. In the first **for loop** line, you'll need to type out from 0 all the way to 35, so it's **for i in [0,1,2,3,... 35]:** and the turn in the last line will be 10 degrees, so it's **alex.right(10)**

11 Finally, insert the two lines shown below into your code from Step 8. You should insert these two after the line **alex = turtle.Turtle()** and before the code for the repeating square. These lines let you add color to your art by changing the pen and background colors.

```
alex.pencolor("yellow")
wn.bgcolor("red")
```

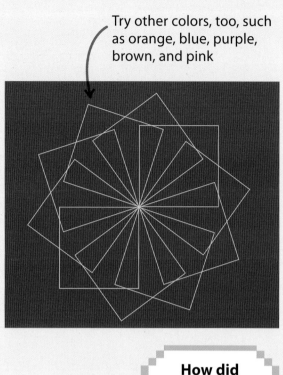

Try other colors, too, such as orange, blue, purple, brown, and pink

Check-in
By changing the number of squares in a pattern and the angle that alex the turtle turns after each square, you can create a range of crazy patterns!

How did your code shape up?

Show what you know
Try these challenges to draw more shapes and patterns.

1. Can you write the code to get your turtle to draw a triangle with equal sides? Use 120-degree turns instead of 90 degrees, and think about how many times you will need to repeat it.

2. Can you use another **for loop** to repeat your triangle and make a pattern? Try the same numbers you used for the square, such as 72 degrees for five turns.

3. Can you create an orange pattern with a blue background?

4. Now try drawing a regular hexagon. It has six sides, and your turtle will need to turn 60 degrees.

Show off!

This project really shows what you can do with a Raspberry Pi. You'll make a piece of artwork that you've created at home or school stand out by using your Raspberry Pi to program small lights, called LEDs, to flash on and off.

Add up to three LEDs to your artwork

Pick one of your favorite pieces of art to show off

Program the LEDs to flash on and off

The Pi and wires are hidden behind the artwork

▲ What you'll do

You will need to open Python 3 (IDLE) for this activity. It can be found under **Programming** on the Raspberry Pi **Menu**. You'll be using a Python library called GPIO Zero, which lets you use the GPIO pins on your Pi. GPIO stands for General Purpose Input/Output, and the pins let you do physical computing projects, such as adding lights in this fun activity.

IMPORTANT
This activity involves building an electronic circuit. When you connect any wires to the GPIO pins on your Pi or make a change to an existing circuit, always make sure that the power is disconnected.

You will also need:

These extras aren't too expensive and can be bought online or from a store. Ask an adult to help you get them.

- **5 to 10 LEDs with built-in resistors (5V)**
Use up to three of these in this project, but have a few spare in case any break.
- **10 female-to-female jumper wires**
Both ends of this type of wire have a hole.
- **2 female-to-male jumper wires**
One end has a hole, and the other end is pointy.
- **An artwork that you want to add LEDs to**
- **Tape**
- **Tinfoil**

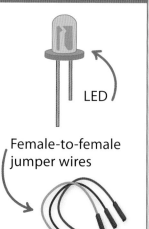
LED

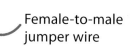
Female-to-female jumper wires

Female-to-male jumper wire

I just love those LEDs!

Meet the GPIO pins!

Before you start programming, you'll need to build a circuit. You should do this before plugging the power into your Raspberry Pi. Your circuit will be connected to the Raspberry Pi using the GPIO pins. These are designed to connect extra things, such as lights, buzzers, and sensors, to your Pi.

GPIO pins are designed to connect to lights, buzzers, sensors, and other devices

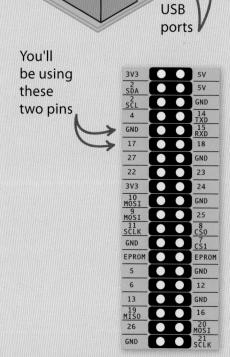
USB ports

It's best to begin by turning your Raspberry Pi so that the USB ports are at the bottom. Now look at this diagram (right), which shows the names of all the pins. The pins might all look the same, but they do different things.

Don't worry about what all of the different pins do. In this project, we'll just use six, starting with Pin 17 and the GND above it. GND stands for Ground, and it is always the end of a circuit. There are several GND pins you can use, and it doesn't really matter which you choose. The pins with numbers can be used for adding accessories, such as the LEDs in this activity.

You'll be using these two pins

3V3	● ●	5V
2 SDA	● ●	5V
2 SCL	● ●	GND
4	● ●	14 TXD
GND	● ●	15 RXD
17	● ●	18
27	● ●	GND
22	● ●	23
3V3	● ●	24
10 MOSI	● ●	GND
9 MOSI	● ●	25
11 SCLK	● ●	8 CS0
GND	● ●	7 CS1
EPROM	● ●	EPROM
5	● ●	GND
6	● ●	12
13	● ●	GND
19 MISO	● ●	16
26	● ●	20 MOSI
GND	● ●	21 SCLK

Building a basic circuit

Before we do anything fancy, we need to make sure we can build a basic circuit and light up one of the LEDs. You will need two female-to-female jumper wires to do this.

1 Attach jumper wires to the two pins shown in the diagram on the opposite page. To do this, just push the pin into the hole. Make sure you count the pins carefully to get the right ones. If you count from the top, there should be nothing on the first four pins on the left side. The next two down will have your jumper wires on.

2 Choose an LED, and look at its legs carefully. Connect the long (positive) leg to the jumper wire on Pin 17, and then connect the short (negative) leg to the jumper wire on GND.

Check-in

You should now have a circuit that connects from Pin 17 to the long leg of the LED and then from the short leg of the LED to GND, to complete the circuit. Check that this is correct, and now connect your Raspberry Pi.

Let there be light!

Helpful hint

It's a good idea to use two differently colored jumper wires. Then it will be easier to remember which one is connected to GND and which one is connected to Pin 17.

The short leg is negative. You can remember this because "–" takes away and the leg has less on it

The long leg is positive. You can remember this because "+" adds and the leg has more added to it

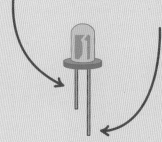

Making your LED light up

When you connect your Pi to the power source, you might expect the LED to light up, but a computer won't do anything without being told. You now need to program it.

Using Python

You are going to program your LED in Python, using a library like you did in the **Crazy patterns** activity. If you haven't done that activity, or can't remember what you did, reread page 25. All the instructions for getting going with Python 3 (IDLE) are also the same for this activity.

Getting started

You'll need some basic commands to get started. You might recognize some of them as being similar to those you used in **Crazy patterns** to program your art.

GPIO Zero is a library (just like the turtle library) and lets you use the GPIO pins. From the GPIO Zero library, you only need the code for LEDs

3 Copy this code. **Remember:** In Python, it's important to copy carefully, including the capital letters. Now run and save the code, as you did in Steps 5–6 on page 27 of **Crazy patterns**, to turn on the LED.

```
from gpiozero import LED

led = LED(17)

led.on()
```

The number in the brackets tells the computer which GPIO pin the LED is plugged into

This line tells the computer to turn on the LED

Give the LED you're using the name **led**

4 The light stays on, unless you tell the Pi to turn it off. To do this, add this line of code and rerun the program.

```
led.off()
```

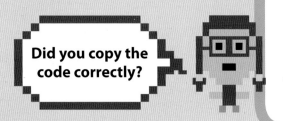

Did you copy the code correctly?

Check-in
Your LED should now light up. If it doesn't, go back and check your jumper wires and that you have copied the code correctly.

Making the light flash

To make the light flash on and off, you need to use another library called **time** and an instruction called **sleep**. This adds a pause in between your instructions, like the **sleep** command you used in Sonic Pi.

The **sleep** instruction comes from the time library. It tells the computer to pause for 1 second before its next command

5 Add the second and fifth lines (below) to your program and then run it. Your LED should now light up and then go off again once.

```
from gpiozero import LED
from time import sleep

led = LED(17)

led.on()
sleep(1)
led.off()
```

6 To keep the LED flashing, you need to use a **while True:** loop. The code you want to repeat goes below this instruction, and it is indented. You indent by pressing the **Tab** key, which is left of the **Q** key.

```
from gpiozero import LED
from time import sleep

led = LED(17)

while True:
    led.on()
    sleep(1)
    led.off()
    sleep(1)
```

Run this code to make the LED flash nonstop

Adding the LED to your artwork

Once you have your circuit working, you can add it to your artwork!

7 Stick your artwork onto a piece of cardboard so that it's stronger and won't rip. Then use a sharp pencil to make a hole where you want the LED to be. When you've made the hole, push the wire legs of the LED through it.

8 When the LED is in place, bend its legs outward on the back of your artwork to stop it from falling out. Then attach the jumper wires, as you did before. **Remember:** The wire from Pin 17 connects to the long (positive) leg. Now run your code.

Check-in
You should now have a light that keeps flashing. **Remember:** You must include two sleep instructions, or you won't notice the loop going back to the beginning.

///////////////////////////////
IMPORTANT
Always disconnect the power each time you change the circuit.
///////////////////////////////

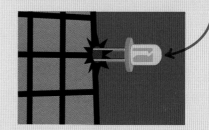

Push LED legs through the hole you made

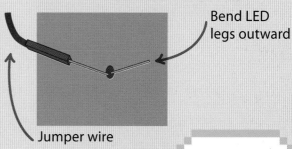

Bend LED legs outward

Jumper wire

Does your light flash?

Check-in
Your light should now flash as part of your artwork. If the wires keep falling off or getting jostled, use some sticky tape to stick them to the back of the picture.

Adding more LEDs

You might now want to use more than one LED to brighten up your artwork. There are two ways that you can do this.

Steps 9–10 tell you how to add more LEDs by using other pins.

Steps 11–15 tell you how to add more LEDs by using the same pair of GPIO pins.

Helpful hint

It's best not to add more than three LEDs to a Pi using the two ways described here. When you have learned the basics of Raspberry Pi, you can then investigate how to create more complicated circuits on special boards called breadboards.

Are you sure you've got enough LEDs?

9 Connect two more LEDs to different GPIO pins, in the same way you did in Steps 1–2. Add one to Pin 18 and the GND below it, and another to Pin 26 and the GND below it. Check the diagram on page 32 for positions.

10 Copy this code and run it. The LEDs should flash in sequence. The advantage of this way is that you can program them all separately, so that they can come off and on at different times.

11 First, pull any wires off the pins. You'll need to connect a male-to-female jumper wire to Pin 17 and another of these wires to the GND pin above it. Leave these two wires for now.

12 Take three LEDs and attach a male-to-female jumper wire to each leg. Make sure you know which legs are positive. For example, you could use red wires for the positive legs and yellow wires for the negative legs.

```python
from gpiozero import LED
from time import sleep

led1 = LED(17)
led2 = LED(18)
led3 = LED(26)

while True:
    led1.on()
    sleep(1)
    led1.off()
    sleep(1)
    led2.on()
    sleep(1)
    led2.off()
    sleep(1)
    led3.on()
    sleep(1)
    led3.off()
    sleep(1)
```

13 Tape the three male ends of the wires coming from the positive legs together, as shown on the right. Do the same with the three ends coming from the negative legs.

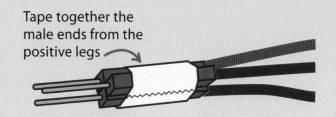
Tape together the male ends from the positive legs

14 Now connect those two bundles of wire ends from the LEDs to the wires attached to the GPIO pins to complete the circuit. **Remember:** The positive legs connect to Pin 17 and the negative legs to GND. You'll need to run the program you wrote in Step 6. The LEDs should now flash at the same time.

Check-in
All three LEDs should now light up. If you get one or two but not all working, give the wires a wiggle as it might be a problem with the connections.

15 If you're having trouble keeping the ends touching, try using tinfoil. Scrunch up two pieces to make two small balls. In one ball, push the ends of the wires from the positive LED legs, as well as the male end of the wire from Pin 17. In the other ball, push the ends of the wires from the negative LED legs, as well as the end of the wire from GND. The tinfoil keeps the ends secure and conducts electricity well.

Show what you know
Now see if you've learned enough to rise to these challenges.

1. Are the following statements true (T) or false (F)?

a. The short leg on an LED is positive. T or F

b. You use just one GPIO pin to light up an LED. T or F

c. Both legs of an LED must be connected to complete the circuit. T or F

d. The ground (GND) pin is connected to the negative leg. T or F

e. You can add more than one LED into the same circuit. T or F

2. Program the lights to come on for 0.5 seconds, go off for 1.5 seconds, go on for 2 seconds, go off for 1 second, and continue to repeat this cycle.

3. Program two LEDs to flash at different times.

Solutions

Check your answers here to the "Challenge" on page 5 and the "Show what you know" sections.

pages 4–5 Raspberry Pi lineup

Project 1: Model A+ **Project 2:** Pi Zero **Project 3:** Pi 3

pages 10–16 Jailbreak

1. **Decomposition** is the word for breaking up a problem into small pieces.
2a. Your instructions sprite might look like this:

> **You've been accidentally sent to jail, and you have 15 seconds to escape before you're locked in for the night. Use the arrow keys to get you to the door. Don't touch the walls or you'll be sent back to the beginning. Click on the space bar to begin.**

Its code should look like this:

You will need to change both of the **when flag clicked** blocks in your robber sprite's scripts to **when space key pressed** blocks, so that the robber only starts doing things (and the timer only starts counting) when you're ready to begin.

2b. Draw a new costume for the door sprite that looks open and name it **Door open**. Name the other door costume **Door closed**.

Name the new costume **Door open**

Name the other costume **Door closed**

Keep the changes you made to the robber sprite's scripts in **2a.** and then program the door sprite to know when it has to change its costume from **Door open** to **Door closed**.

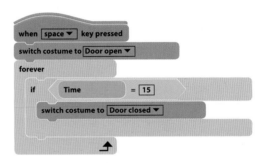

2c. It should be easier to move around using a small robber and trickier to move around using a big robber.

pages 17–23 Sound symphony

1. The notes play "Mary Had a Little Lamb."
2. You will need at least two **live_loops**, one for the chorus and one for the main part of the music. The end of the chorus loop needs the line **sleep 20** so that it waits 20 seconds before repeating. Here's an example:

```
live_loop :beat do
  sample :bass_voxy_hit_c
  sleep 1
  sample :bass_thick_c
end

live_loop :chorus do
  use_synth :pretty_bell
  play 50
  sleep 1
  play 54
  sleep 1
  play 50
  sleep 20
end
```

3. When you make a mistake in Sonic Pi, it gives you a clue at the bottom of the screen to help you correct the mistake. In the first screen, the **sleep** command is missing a number of seconds. In the second screen, you need to give the **live_loop** a name.

4. This code will draw a regular hexagon:

```
for i in [0,1,2,3,4,5]:
    alex.forward(150)
    alex.left(60)
```

pages 24–30 Crazy patterns

Each answer code will need to begin with these lines at the top:

```
import turtle

wn = turtle.Screen()
alex = turtle.Turtle()
```

1. For a triangle, you only need your loop to repeat three times.

```
for i in [0,1,2]:
    alex.forward(150)
    alex.left(120)
```

2. This time you need two loops. One loop will draw your triangle, and the other loop will repeat and turn it a number of times.

```
for i in [0,1,2,3,4]:
    for i in [0,1,2]:
        alex.forward(150)
        alex.left(120)
    alex.right(72)
```

3. You need to set the colors before you program your drawing.

```
alex.pencolor("orange")
wn.bgcolor("blue")
```

pages 31–37 Show off!

1a. False. **1b.** False. **1c.** True. **1d.** True. **1e.** True.
2. Your code should be the following:

```
from gpiozero import LED
from time import sleep

led = LED(17)

while True:
    led.on()
    sleep(0.5)
    led.off()
    sleep(1.5)
    led.on()
    sleep(2)
    led.off()
    sleep(1)
```

3. To make your lights flash at different times, you'll need to use another pair of GPIO pins.

```
from gpiozero import LED
from time import sleep

led1 = LED(17)
led2 = LED(26)

while True:
    led1.on()
    sleep(0.5)
    led2.on()
    led1.off()
    sleep(0.5)
    led2.off()
    sleep(1)
```

Love those crazy patterns!

Updating your Raspberry Pi

Getting your Raspberry Pi connected to the Internet is really useful because you can get any updates that might make it work even better.

Click on the **Wi-Fi** symbol

1. First, click on the **Wi-Fi** symbol at the top of the screen, and select the Wi-Fi network for your home. You will also need to know the Wi-Fi password. If you are unsure, ask an adult for help.

2. Once you're connected to the Internet, you're ready to check if your Pi is up-to-date. To do this, you use something called **Terminal**. Its symbol is a screen. You can find it at the top of your screen. Click on it to open it.

Click on the **Terminal** symbol

3. You will see on a black background the writing: **pi@raspberrypi:~$**. Very carefully copy the writing after the $, shown here in the white box, and press "enter." You may then have to wait some time while your Pi is updated. You will see lots of words scrolling on the screen, telling you about what the Pi is downloading.

pi@raspberrypi:~ $ sudo apt-get update

4. When it's finished downloading, you will again see: **pi@raspberrypi:~$**. Copy the writing after the $, shown here in the white box, and press "enter." Your Pi will now install everything that it has just downloaded. Again, this may take some time.

pi@raspberrypi:~ $ sudo apt-get dist-upgrade

5. You may then be asked something like: **Do you want to continue?** You need to type **Y** (for **yes**) and press "enter." Again, after a short time you will see: **pi@raspberrypi:~$**. It has now finished, and your Pi has been updated.

Type **Y** for **yes** and press "enter"

Do you want to continue? [Y/n]